FROM BEHOLDING
TO BECOMING

FROM BEHOLDING

TO BECOMING

PRAYING THROUGH
THE LIFE
OF CHRIST

KIM COLEMAN HEALY

BrazosPress
Grand Rapids, Michigan

© 2004 by Kim Coleman Healy

Published by Brazos Press
a division of Baker Book House Company
P.O. Box 6287, Grand Rapids, MI 49516-6287
www.brazospress.com

Printed in the United States of America

Library of Congress Cataloging-in-Publication Data
Healy, Kim Coleman, 1963-
    From beholding to becoming : praying through the life of Christ / Kim
Coleman Healy.
        p.   cm.
    Includes bibliographical references.
    ISBN 1-58743-102-5 (cloth)
    1. Jesus Christ—Biography—Devotional literature. I. Title.
BT306.53.H43 2004
232.9'01—dc22   2004003637

Contents

Contents

Acknowledgments

This book owes its being to the efforts of many. The Rev. Lawrence Boadt, C.S.P., recommended crucial structural revisions at a formative stage of the project. The Rev. Dr. Kathryn Greene-McCreight read early versions and introduced me to Brazos Press. I thank Rodney Clapp for accepting the manuscript and Rebecca Cooper and Ruth Goring for expert editing. Melanee McGill, John Hughes, Traci Gresser, Deborah Leslie, and Joshua and Jenny Mosher encouraged me in the transition to full-time writing; my husband Matt provided all manner of moral and material support. Friends at St. John's Episcopal Church, New Haven, Connecticut, listened enthusiastically to prepublication readings.

Introduction

Let the same mind be in you that was in Christ Jesus,
who, though he was in the form of God,
    did not regard equality with God
    as something to be exploited,
but emptied himself,
    taking the form of a slave,
    being born in human likeness.
And being found in human form,
    he humbled himself
    and became obedient to the point of death—
    even death on a cross.

Therefore God also highly exalted him
    and gave him the name
    that is above every name,
so that at the name of Jesus
    every knee should bend,

in heaven and on earth and under the earth,
and every tongue should confess
that Jesus Christ is Lord,
to the glory of God the Father.

Philippians 2:5–11

Why Pray through
the Life of Christ?

*Assist us mercifully with your help, O Lord God of our salvation, that we
may enter with joy upon the contemplation of those mighty acts, whereby
you have given us life and immortality; through Jesus Christ our Lord.
Amen.* (Collect for the Palm Sunday Procession, *The Book of
Common Prayer*)

The incarnation, earthly life, passion, resurrection, and
glorification of Jesus Christ are the preeminent divine
acts that have given us life. In these acts, God has become present in human history. Although we acknowledge Jesus' human
life as a definite historic event, to regard it as mere history can
needlessly impoverish our response. In the resurrection and
ascension, Christ left behind the constraints of created time;
enthroned at the Father's side in the eternal *now* of the kingdom, he promises to be present to us always. This book is an
invitation to encounter Christ's ongoing presence by making
ourselves present to the events of his human story.

Why Should We Meditate on the Life of Christ?

We, like ancient Israel, are enjoined never to forget what God has done for us. By remembering God's deeds we are moved to praise and thank God; indeed, telling what God has done is itself an act of worship. It not only glorifies God but also sustains our hope. When we remind ourselves of what God has done for us in the past, we become more able to trust God for the present and the future. After God answered the prophet Samuel's prayer to deliver Israel from Philistine domination, Samuel set up a monument named Ebenezer, the Stone of Help, saying, "Thus far the LORD has helped us" (1 Sam. 7:12 NRSV[1]). Each of us can sing with the Southern Harmony hymnodist,

> Here I raise mine Ebenezer,
> Hither by Thy help I'm come;

> And I hope by Thy good pleasure
> Safely to arrive at home.[2]

The Ebenezer of the church is the stone that was rolled away from Christ's empty tomb.

When we remember the saving acts of God communally or individually, we are not simply reciting a sacred history lesson. We are making ourselves present to the salvific power that is still present in those acts. Each celebrant of the Passover, from the time of the exodus until now, has enacted the rite "because of what the LORD did *for me* when *I* came out of Egypt" (Exod. 13:8); each Good Friday, when Christians sing, "Were you there when they crucified my Lord?" the implied answer is yes. Whenever we break bread to show forth the Lord's death until he comes, we are in *kairos,* the time of God's action ("When the *fullness of time* had come, God sent his Son, born of a woman, born under the Law," Gal. 4:4), rather than *chronos,* linear human time. We sustain ourselves in the *not yet* of waiting for God's reign by reminding ourselves of how that reign has *already* come.

Praying through the life of Christ will be a familiar concept to readers from liturgical Christian backgrounds. Many Catholics find a sustaining connection to the events of Christ's life by praying the rosary; all liturgical Christians journey communally through the life of Christ in the seasons of the church year. This book has germinated from both of these traditional ways of prayer. However, reflection on the life of Christ is a means of spiritual growth whose usefulness transcends denominational boundaries. The events I meditate on here are all biblical, tracing out the story of redemption that is the common heritage of all Christians.

In the cycle of the liturgical seasons we walk around "the light of the knowledge of the glory of God in the face of Jesus Christ" (2 Cor. 4:6), beholding it from different angles in succession. In the Eucharist we hold up a burning glass to concentrate the redemptive power of the passion and resurrection. But if we are to ignite, we each must place ourselves where the focused beam strikes. Our encounter with God's mighty acts is incomplete until it is internalized. Prayerful engagement with the events of Christ's life can be a major means of internalizing their grace.

Meditating on Christ's life allows us to connect our stories to his story. Beholding Jesus' temptations and sufferings in prayer allows us to know his companionship in our own temptations and sufferings. When we walk with Christ through his valley of the shadow of death, we discover that our own darkness is not dark to him. When we persevere in watching with Christ in his pains, our eyes become opened to see that he has been present in our pains even before we recognized him there. Like the pair walking to Emmaus and the three youths in the fiery furnace, we find that a stranger has joined us; then, suddenly, he is not a stranger at all.

Beholding Christ's resurrection and glory in prayer also brings life and light to whatever needs them in us. Our body, mind, and soul are multilayered, and transmission of his light and warmth from the surface to the interior requires persistent exposure. The dark caverns of our conscious and unconscious mental faculties need to be progressively penetrated by the light of Christ. Prayerful exposure to the mysteries of redemption draws the light down into our labyrinths of darkness, healing and transforming our mind toward conformity with the mind of Christ.

Just as remembering the deeds of God is more than reciting a sacred history lesson, acquiring the mind of Christ is more than imitating a divine role model. Although we humans learn by imitation, we need eventually to go beyond imitation to internalization ("Christ in you, the hope of glory," Col. 1:27) and identification ("I have been crucified with Christ; and it is no longer I who live, but it is Christ who lives in me," Gal. 2:19–20). By beholding the light of Christ through the lens of his self-giving acts, we begin to allow the image of Christ to develop in us. "All of us, with unveiled faces, seeing the glory of the Lord as though reflected in a mirror, are being transformed into the same image from one degree of glory to another; for this comes from the Lord, the Spirit" (2 Cor. 3:18). Beholding leads to becoming.

When we look at Christ as seen in the stories of his life, he looks back at us. His glance may challenge us as it did the rich young ruler, or judge us as it did the hard-hearted opponents of Sabbath healings; it may pierce us as it did Peter at cockcrow or change the world for us as for Mary Magdalene at the empty tomb. Saul's sight of Christ on the Damascus Road destroyed a persecutor and created an apostle.

Paul wrote to the growing Christians in Galatia that he suffered labor pains until Christ was fully formed in them (Gal. 4:19). Beholding Christ in the mysteries of redemption allows his image to implant, grow, develop, and mature within us.

Why "Mysteries"?

In this book, I refer to each event we will ponder as a "mystery." This usage, derived from the rosary and from the medieval mystery plays based on Bible stories, may seem antique and incongruous at first glance. To speak of each event in Christ's life as a *mystery,* however, both acknowledges that we will never plumb the depths of God in Christ and connects each story in the Gospels to the Great Story of God's redemptive plan, formed in Christ before the foundation of the world.

Paul affirms that God's secret wisdom planned from the beginning to make Christ the head of all things.

[God] has made known to us the mystery of his will, according to his good pleasure that he set forth in Christ, as a plan for the fullness of time, to gather up all things in him, things in heaven and things on earth. (Eph. 1:9–10)

Christ's coming in the flesh opened the secret to those with the eyes to recognize him; his resurrection and ascension showed the secret forth to the entire cosmos.

The secrets that Jesus told his disciples in the dark, in whispers, in parables, became the good news that when shouted from the housetops turned their world upside down. After Jesus' ascension, the same process is carried on by the Spirit, revealing God's mysteries to the hearts of the faithful. Over and over Paul prays that the readers of his letters will come to comprehend the secrets of God's gracious purpose manifested in Christ. The Amplified Version renders his prayer for the Ephesians like this:

> [For I always pray to] the God of our Lord Jesus Christ, the Father of glory, that He may grant you a spirit of wisdom and revelation [of insight into mysteries and secrets] in the [deep and intimate] knowledge of Him, by having the eyes of your heart flooded with light, so that you can know and understand the hope to which He has called you and how rich is His glorious inheritance in the saints (His set-apart ones). (Eph. 1:17–18 AMP)

When we open our hearts to Jesus' continuing self-disclosure through the Spirit, he prepares a place for himself in us; this indwelling is the culminating mystery of our salvation.

Our internal, lived understanding of the saving acts of God and our receptivity to Christ's presence in us then can turn outward, unpacking the riches of the secret for others. St. Thomas Aquinas affirmed that the highest Christian calling is *contemplata tradere,* sharing the fruits of contemplation.

When we tell Christ's story from our own lived experience of it, our hearers will find themselves drawn into the story as well.

How to Use This Book

Each mystery is introduced by a brief reflection. These reflections are catalysts; they are meant to stimulate your own prayerful imagination, not to displace it. Each is accompanied by a primary Scripture reference and followed by a brief prayer response; a selection of additional Scripture references is provided for further meditation. (Occasionally verse divisions in the Psalms differ among translations. My references are based on the Psalter of the 1979 *Book of Common Prayer*.)

When reading this material devotionally, *don't rush!* The text functions less as a source of information than as an icon, a window opening into the presence of God, where you are invited to be still. You can use one chapter or selection daily, or one selection in the morning and one in the evening; read the Scripture passage along with the text reflection. Read slowly; breathe deeply; pause often. Don't hesitate to reread. When a particular word or phrase in the Scripture or the text strikes a chord, you may wish to linger over it, repeating it silently until you have absorbed and responded to it, in the ancient practice known as *lectio divina.* The concluding response provided in the text may be prayed aloud if desired.

After reading a mystery, you may choose to continue meditating on it while maintaining focus by means of a brief repeated prayer. A suggested prayer introduces each chapter. Its opening couplet, "Blessed be Jesus Christ, very God and very man. Blessed be the holy name of Jesus," has been adopted from Austin Farrer's *Lord I Believe*[3] and is followed by a scriptural or traditional couplet appropriate to the chapter's theme. Alternatively, the Jesus Prayer, "Lord Jesus Christ, Son of God, have mercy on me, a sinner," or the Trisagion, "Holy God, Holy and Mighty, Holy Immortal One, have mercy upon us," may be used.

If you are accustomed to praying the rosary, you will find that each chapter of five mysteries fits into a complete circuit of the beads; the chapter prayer, Jesus Prayer, or Trisagion may be used as the primary repeated prayer. You may wish to read the text of each mystery between the Our Father and the decade prayers; alternatively, the entire chapter can be read beforehand, then its themes freely pondered during the prayer.

If a certain mystery captures your attention, it may point to an event of Christ's life that offers a specific grace you need. Feel free to return to any selection as often as you desire; each selection includes enough suggested Scriptures to support many prayer periods. Appropriately selected mysteries can be used to enrich a particular celebration (Christmas, Easter, Pentecost) or season; however, the glorified Christ dwells in *kairos* rather than *chronos,* and so any of the mysteries can be prayed at any time.

The order of the mysteries roughly corresponds to the order of events in the Gospels. The Mysteries of Joy commemorate the beginning of Christ's incarnate life: Gabriel's announcement of the coming birth to Mary, her visit to Elizabeth, Jesus' birth, his presentation to Simeon and Anna in the temple, and Jesus at twelve, lost and found with the temple scholars. In these stories we behold the Word's descent into infancy and learn with Mary to nurture his growth in our lives.

The Mysteries of Manifestation begin Jesus' adult ministry: his baptism in the Jordan, his desert temptation, his call of Simon Peter, his first miracle at Cana, and his preaching in the synagogue of Nazareth. Here we are challenged by his authority and claimed by his call.

The Mysteries of Healing invite us, with a leper, a centurion's servant, a man with a withered hand, a woman suffering hemorrhage, and the twelve-year-old daughter of Jairus, to bring all our ills to the Great Physician.

The Mysteries of Mercy show Jesus' power to forgive sins. In the stories of how he forgave a paralytic, a house party of tax collectors, a prostitute who anointed his feet, a Samaritan woman, and an adulterous woman under sentence of death, we rediscover his forgiveness extended to us.

The Mysteries of Growth place us in Jesus' botanical parables. The images—sower, seed, and soil, weeds among the wheat, mustard seeds and yeast, sparrows and lilies, vines and fig trees—call us to acknowledge Christ's power to make us grow.

The Mysteries of Power call us to adore Jesus' divine reign over creation: feeding multitudes, calming the sea, casting out demons, making new eyes for one born blind, showing his transfigured glory.

The Mysteries of the Kingdom connect us to characters in the parables of the wedding banquet, the unjust judge, the vineyard workers, the talents, and the wicked tenants. These stories show God's ways turning the world upside down.

The Mysteries of Jerusalem carry us through the last week of Jesus' life, witnessing his anointing at Bethany, the triumphal entry, Jesus' weeping over Jerusalem, the cleansing of the temple, and the Last Supper.

The Mysteries of Sorrow—the agony in the garden, the scourging under Pilate, the crowning with thorns, the way of the cross, and the crucifixion—put Jesus' sufferings before us. Descending into our merited punishment, he refuses to be absent from anywhere our exile has taken us.

The Mysteries of Glory call us to exalt Jesus' unending life: the resurrection, the ascension, the sending of the Holy Spirit at Pentecost, Jesus' high priesthood, and his promised return.

May these reflections increase your insight into the mystery hidden in God's plan for eons but now revealed to God's people: Christ in you, the hope of glory (Col. 1:26–27).

Mysteries of Joy

Blessed be Jesus Christ, very God and very Man.
Blessed be the holy name of Jesus!
The Word was made flesh and dwelt among us,
And we beheld his glory, full of grace and truth.

The Annunciation

In my prayer corner, two icons sit side by side. On the right, the unborn Jesus reigns from within Mary's womb, surrounded by an amniotic circle of night sky blazing with stars. On the left, Dame Julian of Norwich cups a hazelnut in her palm; in her vision, shown as an inset, the hands of Christ cup the earth and moon as seen from space.

The juxtaposition of these icons captures for me the paradox of the annunciation. The Word who holds the stars in their courses now leaps down from his royal throne. The Son who made all things visible and invisible now descends through all ranks of creatures into a single cell. The One who contains the expanding universe now wills to *be* contained in Mary's womb.

Bernard of Clairvaux (1090–1153) imagines all generations as waiting in suspense for Mary's answer to Gabriel's invitation.

> Tearful Adam with his sorrowing family begs this of you, O loving Virgin, in their exile from Paradise. Abraham begs it, David begs it. All the other holy patriarchs, your ancestors, ask it of you, as they dwell in the country of the shadow of death.

Open your heart to faith, O blessed Virgin, your lips to praise, your womb to the Creator. See, the desired of all nations is at your door, knocking to enter.[1]

The Word comes to his own: will she receive him, and so give to all people the power to become children of God? "Here am I, the servant of the Lord; let it be with me according to your word." For her consent, all generations from Adam forward call her blessed.

Because Mary opened her door to the One desired by all nations, Jesus came to say, "Listen! I am standing at the door, knocking; if you hear my voice and open the door, I will come in to you and eat with you, and you with me" (Rev. 3:20). As Mary made a place for God in her womb, we are called to make a place for God in our inner self.

The ultimate dwelling place of God will be the Church Triumphant. No temple will be needed in the New Jerusalem, because its citizens will have known the indwelling of the Lord God Almighty and the Lamb from the first moment of their consent. As patriarchs and prophets waited for Mary's yes, so the great cloud of witnesses waits for ours.

Response

When all things were in quiet silence, and night was in the midst of her swift course, your Almighty Word, O Lord, leaped down out of your royal throne. Alleluia!

Traditional antiphon from Christmas Vespers[2]

For Further Meditation

Matthew 1:18–25 (Mary's conception and Joseph's acceptance)
John 1:1–18 (The Word became flesh and lived among us)
Psalm 2 (You are my son; today I have begotten you!)
Psalm 132 (David's vow to make a place for God)

The Visitation

LUKE 1:39—56

I imagine Mary's sharp intake of breath as she realizes afresh, several times an hour, just what is within her now. On her journey to Elizabeth's home, the energetic gait of a healthy teenager alternates with pauses to feel her belly and blink, to move slowly for the sake of the Promised One within. Mary travels to her kinswoman's side with both the urgency of one impelled by the Spirit and the tender caution of one who has just conceived by the Spirit.

Elizabeth, meanwhile, has practiced her own tender caution through five months of seclusion, pondering God's acts with a quiet attention that Mary will come to emulate. Her solitude and silence have formed a protective environment for the image of God developing in her son. We can learn from the tender caution of Mary and Elizabeth to nurture the fragile work of God within us, which grows in its own time whether we see and feel it or not.

Jesus, growing within Mary, is too young yet for quickening; John the Baptist is six months along and kicking. The Eastern Orthodox Akathist Hymn paints a charming picture of John's leap of recognition as Mary, bearing Jesus, greets Elizabeth:

> Pregnant with God, the Virgin hastened to Elizabeth, her
>   unborn child rejoiced, immediately knowing her
>   embrace. Bouncing and singing, he cried out to the
>   Mother of God:
> Hail, O Tendril whose Bud shall not wilt!

Hail, O Soil whose Fruit shall not perish!
Hail, O Tender of mankind's loving Tender!
Hail, O Gardener of the Gardener of Life![3]

The fructifying power of God, which Elizabeth accepted in faith despite her own and Zechariah's doubt, has become living, leaping reality. Elizabeth's conception brings lifelong barrenness into sudden flower; Mary's conception brings supernatural fruit from unplowed ground.

We are called, with Mary and Elizabeth, to take seriously the task of gestating what God gives us to bring forth. My favorite image for this comes from a Lois McMaster Bujold novel. Cordelia Vorkosigan, "gestating assiduously" with her first child, "purred an encouraging mental mantra bellywards, *Grow, grow, grow.*"[4] May we, whatever our gender, constantly say "Grow, grow, grow!" to the implanted Word.

Response

May the Son of God who is formed in you grow strong and immense in you and become for you great gladness and exaltation and perfect joy.

Blessed Isaac of Stella (1105–1178)[5]

For Further Meditation

1 Samuel 2:1–10 (Hannah's song—a poem echoed by Mary's Magnificat)
Psalm 139:13–16 (You knit me together in my mother's womb)
Ecclesiastes 11:5 (You do not know how the bones grow in the womb)
Matthew 13:31–32 (The mustard seed)
Isaiah 54:1 (Exult, O barren one!)

The Nativity

LUKE 2:1—20

Young Mary endures Eve's travails in a body for which even menstrual cramps are a recent discovery. When Jesus at last emerges, Mary can say with Eve, "I have produced a man with the help of the LORD!" (Gen. 4:1). Jesus' first wail is a battle cry of the Seed of Eve against the serpent whose head he has come to bruise.

> Out of the mouths of infants and children
> > your majesty is praised above the heavens.
> You have set up a stronghold against your adversaries,
> > to quell the enemy and the avenger.
> When I consider your heavens, the work of your fingers,
> > the moon and the stars you have set in their courses,
> What is man that you should be mindful of him?
> > the son of man that you should seek him out?

> Psalm 8:2—5

This Son of Man is Son of God, now lower than the angels, looking up to the stars of his handiwork with eyes that cannot yet fully focus.

The Word who holds all things in being now depends utterly on the secure holding of his mother and father. Mary wraps